REAL WORLD
MATHS

treasure
in the
JUNGLE

Wendy Clemson and Frances Clemson

© TickTock Entertainment Ltd 2007, 2011
This revised edition published in 2011 by TickTock.
First published in Great Britain as
Using Maths Treasure in the Jungle in 2007 by TickTock.
The Pantiles Chambers, 85 High Street,
Tunbridge Wells, Kent, TN1 1XP, UK.

ISBN 978 1 84898 536 0

Printed in China
10 9 8 7 6 5 4 3 2 1

With thanks to our consultant Kerry Johnson, who supplied revisions
for this latest book, ensuring all material is current.

Picture Credits
t=top, b=bottom, c=centre, l=left, r=right, f=far
Amazon-Images/Alamy: 2, 19t. Wolfgang Kaehler/Alamy: 11. Yann Arthus-Bertrand/Corbis: 29. e.t. archive: 1.
Shutterstock: front cover, 3c, 3fl, 4tl, 4tr, 4bl, 4br, 5, 7, 8, 9, 10, 13, 14, 15, 16t, 16c, 16b,
17t, 17b, 18, 19b, 20, 21, 22, 23, 24-25, 27, 30, 31b, 31t, 32.
Werner Forman Archive: 6b. Ticktock Media Archive: 6t
BFL e.t. archive. Back cover: TL and BR Shutterstock.

Every effort has been made to trace the copyright holders and we apologise in advance for any unintentional omissions.
We would be pleased to insert the appropriate acknowledgement in any subsequent edition of this publication.

Contents

Be an Explorer 4

Looking for Treasure! 6

Off to Peru 8

Ready for the Expedition 10

The Treasure Map 12

High in the Mountains 14

Into the Jungle 16

On the Jungle Floor 18

Jungle Butterflies and Birds 20

Discovering the Temple 22

Inside the Temple 24

Temple Treasures 26

Patterns and Pictures 28

Tips and Help 30

Answers 32

NUMERACY WORK COVERED IN THIS BOOK:

Numbers and the number system
Rounding: pgs 6-7
Place value: pgs 8-9
Odds and evens: pgs 16-17
Putting numbers in order: pgs 18-19
Fractions: pgs 24-25

Shape, space and measurements
Telling the Time: pgs 8-9
Flat shapes: pgs 10-11
Compass N, S, E and W: pgs 12-13
Kilometre: pgs 12-13
Measuring length: pgs 14-15
Estimates: pgs 18-19
Measuring with a ruler: pgs 20-21
Solid shapes: pgs 22-23
Angles: pgs 28-29

Organising data
Venn diagram (sorting): pgs 10-11
Calculation signs: pgs 16-17
Pictogram: pgs 26-27

Problem solving
Predicting patterns: pgs 24-25

Mental calculations
Groups of 10: pg 6
Addition, subtraction and multiplication: pgs 17, 19 and 21
Counting and difference: pg 18

Supports the maths work taught at Key Stage 1/2

Be an Explorer

You are an explorer. You travel all over the world. Explorers find amazing places that very few people have ever seen. Today you are going on an exciting adventure to search for hidden treasure. If you find some treasure you will give it to a museum so that everyone can see it!

Being an explorer can be dangerous, but it can also be great fun!

Explorers climb mountains and trek through jungles.

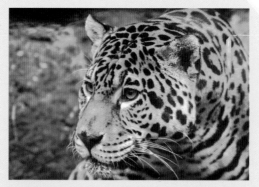

Sometimes explorers see unusual wild animals!

Explorers find treasures and ancient ruins that tell us about the past.

They sometimes have to camp in very hot or cold places.

But did you know that explorers sometimes have to use maths?

In this book you will find lots of number puzzles that explorers have to solve to help them find out about secret places and treasures. You will also get the chance to answer lots of number questions about the things you see.

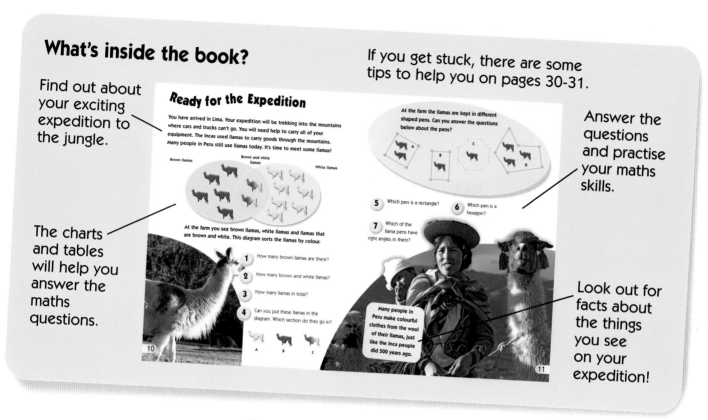

What's inside the book?

Find out about your exciting expedition to the jungle.

The charts and tables will help you answer the maths questions.

If you get stuck, there are some tips to help you on pages 30-31.

Answer the questions and practise your maths skills.

Look out for facts about the things you see on your expedition!

Ready for the Expedition

You have arrived in Lima. Your expedition will be trekking into the mountains where cars and trucks can't go. You will need help to carry all of your equipment. The Incas used llamas to carry goods through the mountains. Many people in Peru still use llamas today. It's time to meet some llamas!

Brown llamas
Brown and white llamas
White llamas

At the farm you see brown llamas, white llamas and llamas that are brown and white. This diagram sorts the llamas by colour.

1. How many brown llamas are there?
2. How many brown and white llamas?
3. How many llamas in total?
4. Can you put these llamas in the diagram. Which section do they go in?

A   B   C

10

At the farm the llamas are kept in different shaped pens. Can you answer the questions below about the pens?

A   B   C   D

5. Which pen is a rectangle?
6. Which pen is a hexagon?
7. Which of the llama pens have right angles in them?

Many people in Peru make colourful clothes from the wool of their llamas, just like the Inca people did 500 years ago.

11

Are you ready to be an explorer?

You will need paper, a pencil, a ruler and don't forget to bring your equipment! Let's go...

Looking for Treasure!

You are going on a trip to a country in South America called Peru. On your adventure you will climb mountains and explore thick, dark jungle. You will see ruins and lots of unusual animals. If you are lucky you hope to find Inca treasure hidden in the jungle to give to a museum in Peru!

The Inca people lived in Peru about 500 years ago. This is an Inca picture of ten warriors.

1 The Inca kings put their people into groups of 10, 100 and 1000. This made it easier for the kings to organise them. How many groups of 10 in 40?

2 How many groups of 10 are there in 110?

3 If you put 82 people into groups of 10, how many groups of 10 will there be?

4 How many people will be left over?

This is a gold Inca mask. The Incas had lots of gold and silver treasure.

5 Round each of these numbers to the nearest 10:

33   65   78   40   96

6 Which of these numbers have a 5 in the hundreds place:

35   579   56   1509   1536

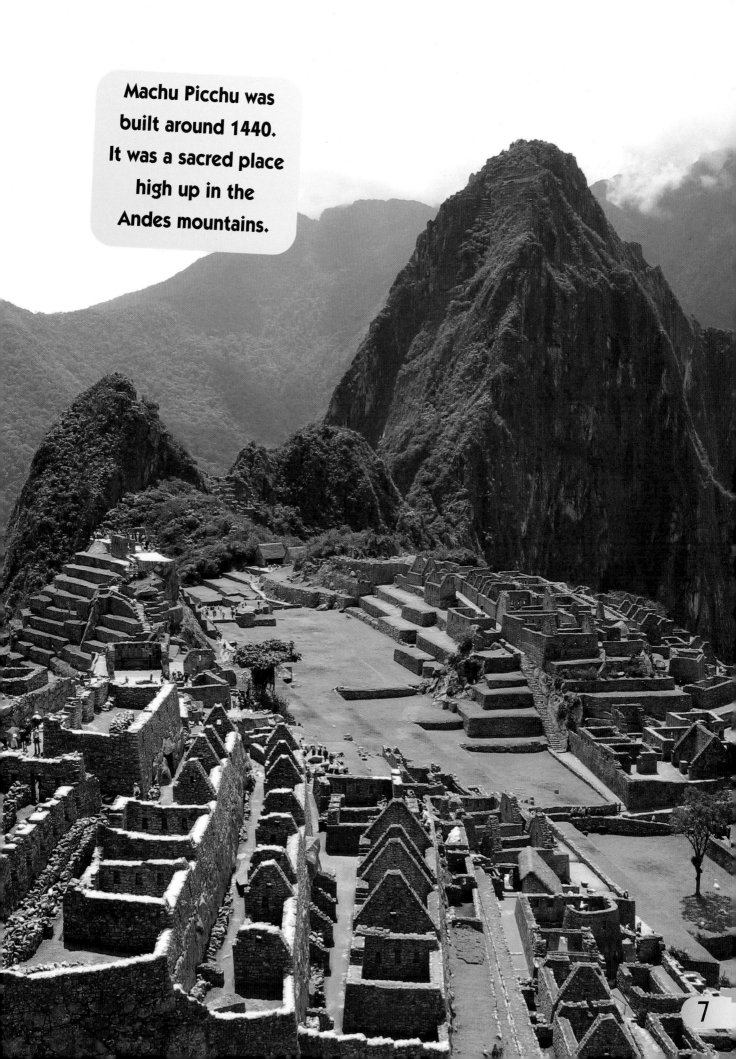

Machu Picchu was built around 1440. It was a sacred place high up in the Andes mountains.

Off to Peru

You are leading a team of explorers. The members of your team are coming from all over the world. Some of them have a long plane journey to reach Peru. You will meet the other explorers in Lima, the capital city of Peru.

FLIGHT TIMES TO LIMA

Leaving from		Going to	Time it will take
London	United Kingdom	Lima, Peru	17 hours
Washington, D.C.	United States	Lima, Peru	11 hours
Moscow	Russia	Lima, Peru	21 hours
Mexico City	Mexico	Lima, Peru	6 hours
Nairobi	Kenya	Lima, Peru	29 hours

1 Look at the flight times chart. How long does it take to get from Washington, D.C. to Lima?

2 How long does it take to get from Moscow to Lima?

3 Which journey takes the least time?

4 Which journey takes longer than a day?

8

To get to Lima you must fly over the Andes Mountains.
The Andes are the longest mountain range in the world.
The mountains stretch for 8,800 kilometres!

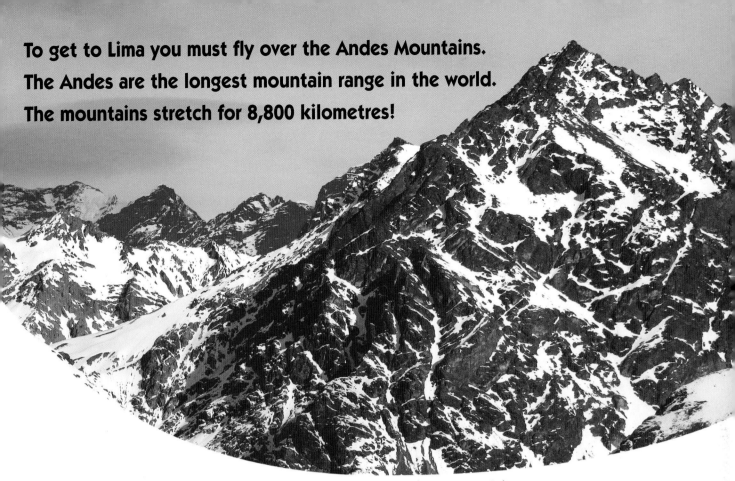

Use the flight times chart to answer the questions on this page.

5 If you leave Washington, D.C. at 12:00 which clock shows your arrival time?

A

B

C

6 If an explorer leaves Mexico City at 3:00 which clock shows his arrival time?

A

B

C

9

Ready for the Expedition

You have arrived in Lima. Your expedition will be trekking into the mountains where cars and trucks can't go. You will need help to carry all of your equipment. The Incas used llamas to carry goods through the mountains. Many people in Peru still use llamas today. It's time to meet some llamas!

Brown llamas　　　**Brown and white llamas**　　　**White llamas**

At the farm you see brown llamas, white llamas and llamas that are brown and white. This diagram sorts the llamas by colour.

1 How many brown llamas are there?

2 How many brown and white llamas?

3 How many llamas in total?

4 Can you put these llamas in the diagram. Which section do they go in?

A　　　B　　　C

At the farm the llamas are kept in different shaped pens. Can you answer the questions below about the pens?

5 Which pen is a rectangle?

6 Which pen is a hexagon?

7 Which of the llama pens have right angles in them?

Many people in Peru make colourful clothes from the wool of their llamas, just like the Inca people did 500 years ago.

The Treasure Map

You're off to look for an Inca temple hidden deep in the jungle. No other explorer has been able to find the temple, but you have an old map that shows you where the temple might be! The first part of your journey will be through the mountains using stony roads built by the Inca people.

TREASURE MAP

MAP KEY

pool	
swamp	
mountains	
rare flowers	
temple	
jungle	
statue	

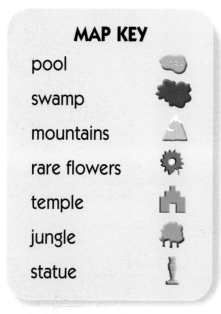

Look at the treasure map. True or false?

1 The jungle is north of the rare flowers.

2 The mountains are east of the temple.

3 The pool is east of the swamp.

12

Look at the treasure map again. Where will you end up if you follow these directions?

4 Start at the statue. Go two squares right and two squares up.

5 Start at the swamp. Go four squares right and two squares down.

6 Start at the pool. Go one square down. Go two squares left and then down one square.

7 The Incas didn't have horses, so everything was carried by people or llamas. The Incas built good roads. Would you use centimetres or metres to measure the width of a stone on an Inca road?

8 Would you use centimetres or kilometres to measure the length of an Inca road?

The Incas built roads to help people travel around Peru. Some roads went from one end of their kingdom to the other.

13

High in the Mountains

Being an explorer can be very tough! You are trekking along rocky, mountain roads. When you are high up in the mountains the air is thinner. This makes it hard to breathe, and it can make you feel sick! Thankfully you planned your trip for May when it is not too hot or too cold in Peru.

1 Look at the months of the year. Can you put them in the right order?

2 If the expedition lasts to the end of May, what month will it be when you go home?

MONTHS OF THE YEAR

May	April	September
June	August	January
July	October	November
February	December	March

WOW! You have just spotted a condor. The condor is one of the biggest birds in the world. These giant birds live high in the Andes mountains.

Condors don't flap their wings very often. Instead they glide on their huge wings as they look for food.

The condor's wings measure 3 metres from tip to tip.

3 How many centimetres in one metre?

4 How many centimetres in half a metre?

5 How many centimetres in 3 metres?

6 Is ¼ metre more or less than 30 centimetres?

Into the Jungle

You are following the treasure map into the jungle. Explorers take photographs and make notes about everything they see on an expedition. The jungle is full of unusual animals to look out for. What's that noise? It's a fierce, fast big cat called a jaguar!

1 Jaguars are covered in spots. This makes it hard for other animals to see them when they are hunting in the shady jungle. Which of the three jaguars below has an odd number of spots?

A   B   C

2 Which have even numbers of spots?

3 Which one has the fewest spots?

4 Which jaguar has the most spots?

5 Is 3 an odd or an even number?

6 Everywhere you look in the jungle you see little squirrel monkeys. How many can you count on these pages?

Squirrel monkeys live in groups called troops. There are normally 40 to 50 monkeys in one troop. But sometimes there can be 200!

7 Now try these monkey puzzles!

A 2 monkeys + 2 monkeys + 2 monkeys

B 3 x 2 monkeys

C 2 monkeys + 6 monkeys

D 4 monkeys - 2 monkeys

E 2 x 2 monkeys

On the Jungle Floor

On the ground there are thousands of tiny insects and jungle creatures. Look – leafcutter ants! The ants are collecting pieces of leaf and taking them back to their nest. They use the leaves to make a special ant food.

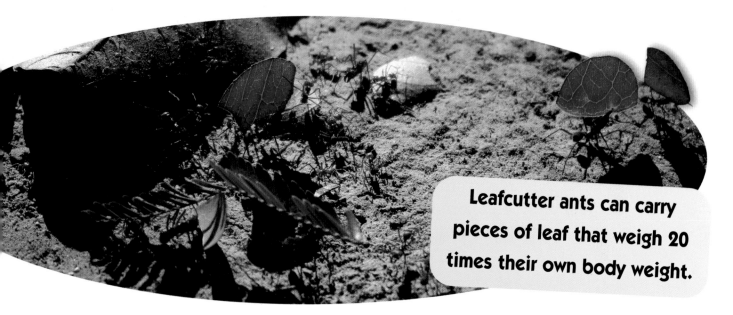

Leafcutter ants can carry pieces of leaf that weigh 20 times their own body weight.

1 Look at the group of leafcutter ants in the box. Estimate how many there are and write it down. Now count the ants. What is the difference between your estimate and the actual number of ants?

2 How many ants are there rounded to the nearest ten?

You spot a tiny poison dart frog. These frogs have deadly, poisonous skin that stops snakes and big spiders eating them!

This poison dart frog is only 1 centimetre long.

Poison dart frogs come in lots of different colours. Try these frog additions:

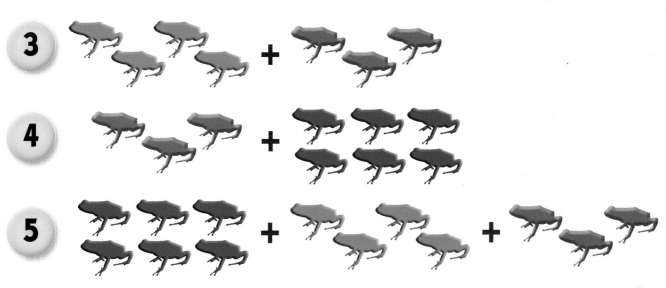

3

4

5

6 Millipedes live in the jungle too. 'Millipede' means '1000 feet' but most millipedes only have between 80 and 400 feet. Which of these numbers are between 80 and 400?

66	81
42	300
93	88
410	100

Jungle Butterflies and Birds

You have now been trekking through the jungle for five days! You walk for about 16 kilometres every day. Your explorer's notebook is filling up with notes about exciting jungle creatures!

EXPLORER'S NOTEBOOK

Jungle creatures	Number spotted
Jaguars	3
Blue poison dart frogs	10
Millipedes	9
Blue morpho butterflies	16
Red poison dart frogs	22

1 Look at the explorer's notebook. How many millipedes have you seen?

2 Which creature have you seen 16 of?

3 How many poison dart frogs have you seen in total?

4 This is a blue morpho butterfly. This giant butterfly lives in the jungles of South America. Use your ruler to measure the butterfly's wingspan. How many centimetres does the butterfly measure?

5 You spot a toucan up in the trees. Its huge orange beak is 20 centimetres long. Its body is 64 centimetres long. Can you do these puzzles using 20 and 64?

64 + 20

20 + 20

64 – 20

64 + 64

Toucans are not very good at flying. They hop from tree branch to tree branch!

Discovering the Temple

Suddenly through the thick trees and bushes you spot the ruins of a building. The map was right! You have found an Inca temple. The Incas had lots of different gods including a sun god. They built temples as special places to make their sun god happy.

The Incas did not have mortar to glue stones together. Their walls were built with stones that fitted together well.

1 Which of these shapes would be good for building?

A

B

C

D

2 Can you match these names to the shapes?

Cylinder **Cube** **Sphere** **Pyramid**

These bricks will be used to build a large triangle shape. Here are the bottom two rows.

3 How many bricks should be in the next row up? How many bricks in the row after that?

4 How many bricks will be at the top of the triangle?

5 Now try this brick pattern. A wall has **30 bricks**, then **25 bricks**, then **20 bricks**. What comes next?

Inside the Temple

The Incas' kingdom measured about 5000 kilometres from one end to the other. The land was divided into four parts and named "Tawantinsuyu". This Inca word means "Land of the four quarters". You decide to split up your team of explorers into four groups to explore the temple.

Temple plan A

Temple plan B

Temple plan C

Temple plan E

Temple plan D

1 Look at these plans of the temple. Some of them have been divided into quarters. Which ones?

2 How many sections has Plan B been divided into?

3 Which is bigger two halves or two quarters?

4 How many quarters do you need to make one half?

There is no writing on the walls of the temple. The Inca people did not know how to write. Instead of writing they tied knots in pieces of string. Different numbers of knots gave different messages.

Look at these knot patterns. How many knots come next on each string?

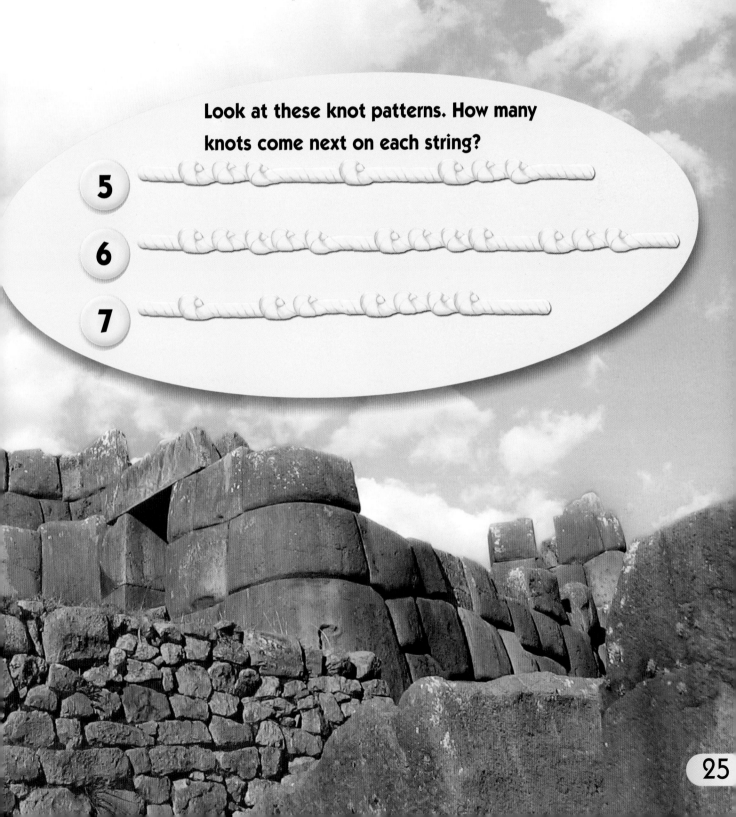

5

6

7

Temple Treasures

There are lots of wonderful treasures in the temple. The Inca kings were very rich. Their people made things from gold and silver dug out of the ground. They used these metals and copper and bronze, along with stone, pottery and wood. They made statues, drinking and cooking pots and jewellery.

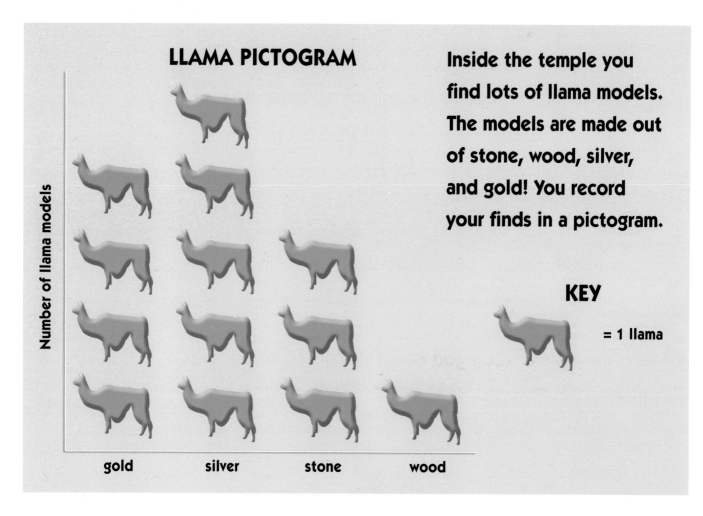

LLAMA PICTOGRAM

Number of llama models

gold   silver   stone   wood

Inside the temple you find lots of llama models. The models are made out of stone, wood, silver, and gold! You record your finds in a pictogram.

KEY

= 1 llama

Use the pictogram to answer these questions:

1 How many gold llama models are there?

2 How many more silver llamas than gold llamas?

3 How many more gold llamas than wood llamas?

4 How many llama models did you find in total?

The llamas will have lots of exciting things to carry back to the museum in Lima. They take a rest in the temple ruins!

The Inca's sun god was called Inti and they had a moon god called Quilla.
You find lots of model suns and moons in the temple. Count them!

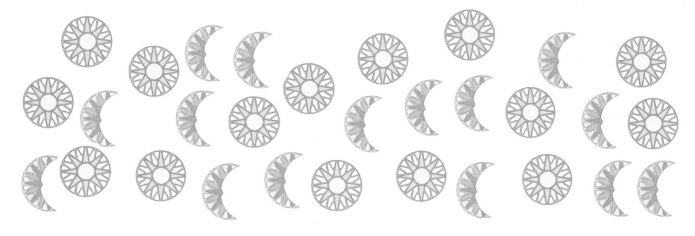

5 You need to pack them up into boxes of ten. How many groups of ten can you make?

6 The sun and moon models weigh 2 kilograms each. If a llama can carry 20 kilograms on its back, how many llamas do you need to carry the sun and moon models?

Patterns and Pictures

The Incas liked to use patterns, squares and right angles to decorate their things. On the way home from your expedition you will fly over some giant pictures and patterns called the Nazca lines. They were drawn in the desert sand by people who lived in Peru 2000 years ago!

1 We call this a chequerboard pattern. The Incas used it a lot. What numbers would you find in the bottom row of the chequerboard?

2 Would the numbers below be on red or yellow squares?
8   11   17   20

3 Numbers in the 2 x table all fall on the same colour square. Is that red or yellow?

This is an Inca pattern called a "tocapus". These patterns are found on material. The Incas were very good at weaving.

4 Look at these patterns. Trace the outside of each shape with your finger. How many right angles do you move through?

A

B

C

The Nazca drawings include animals, insects, birds and patterns. As your plane flies over a giant spider drawing you can see it from different directions.

Look at the spider. Your plane is going around clockwise.

A

B

C

5 Which picture shows the spider after a quarter turn?

6 Which picture shows the spider after a half turn?

This Nazca spider is 40 metres long! It is just one of the amazing things you have seen on your expedition in Peru!

Tips and Help

PAGES 6-7

Rounding – When we round a number to the nearest ten we make a number ending in 5, 6, 7, 8 or 9 bigger and numbers ending in 1, 2, 3 or 4 smaller. So 33 rounded to the nearest ten is 30 whereas 65 becomes 70 because it is rounded up.

Place value – We use only nine symbols to write all numbers. The 'place' of each symbol gives it 'value'. For example, 579 has a '5' in the hundreds 'place', '7' in the tens 'place' and '9' in the ones 'place', so we read this number as five hundred and seventy nine.

PAGES 8-9

Telling the Time – When the longer hand on a clock is pointing at 'twelve' the time is 'o'clock'. The shorter hand on a clock is the hour hand. It tells us what o'clock it is.

PAGES 10-11

Sorting – This is called a Venn diagram. It shows a set of brown llamas and white llamas. The sets overlap so that the llamas that are mixed (both brown and white) are in the brown set and the white set.

Flat shapes – Counting the sides is necessary in naming flat shapes. A hexagon has six sides, an octagon eight sides, a rectangle four sides (opposite sides match in length) and four right angles and a square four sides of equal length and four right angles.

PAGES 12-13

Compass N, S, E, and W – (North, South, East and West) are called the points of the compass. A compass shows which direction is North. It can help us find our way.

Kilometre – One kilometre is 1000 metres.

PAGES 14-15

Month – There are 12 months in a year.

Measuring length – There are 100 centimetres in one metre.

PAGES 16-17

Odds and evens – Even numbers are in the pattern of counting in twos: 2 4 6 8 and so on. Odd numbers are those that are not even: 1 3 5 7 9 and so on.

Calculation signs – Remember that + means add, – means subtract, x means multiply.

PAGES 18-19

Estimate – An estimate can be made when we look at all the information we have and decide what an answer is likely to be. It is very important in mathematics as we can judge whether an answer we have is probably the correct one.

Putting numbers in order – To put these numbers in order starting with the lowest number, try looking at the numbers that are just 'tens' and 'ones' first. 42 has fewest tens and so this is the lowest number. When you have all the 'tens' and ones' numbers in order, look for the number with the fewest 'hundreds' and so on. Then look at your number line and mark where 80 and 400 come. The numbers between 80 and 400 are the answers.

PAGES 20-21

Measuring with a ruler – Be careful to place the ruler so that the '0' (zero) is exactly on one end of the line to be measured. Then you can 'read off' the width of the wingspan of the butterfly at the other end of the line.

PAGES 22-23

Solid shapes – A sphere is a perfectly round ball. A cube has 6 square faces and 8 corners. A pyramid has a square base, four faces that are triangles and it comes to a 'point' called the apex. A cylinder has 1 flat side that wraps around and joins to the 2 identical circles on the end.

PAGES 24-25

Fractions – A fraction is part of a whole. When we share or cut something into four equal parts each is ¼ (a quarter). If it is cut into two equal parts, each part is the fraction ½ (half).

Predicting patterns – When we work out how a pattern would continue we are predicting (deciding what will happen). Count the knots, look for a pattern; and then imagine that the same pattern goes on across the page.

PAGES 26-27

Pictogram – This is a chart where a picture is used as a symbol for information. In this pictogram a llama shape means 1 llama.

PAGES 28-29

Right angle – There are four right angles in a complete turn. A right angle is often shown like this:

right angle

A quarter turn – There are four quarter turns in one complete turn. Each quarter turn is a turn through a right angle.

Answers

PAGES 6-7

1 4
2 11
3 8 groups
4 2 people left over
5 30 70 80 40 100
6 579, 1509 and 1536

PAGES 8-9

1 11 hours
2 21 hours
3 Mexico City to Lima
4 Nairobi to Lima
5 Clock C
6 Clock A

PAGES 10-11

1 5 brown llamas
2 2 brown and white llamas
3 14 llamas
4 A - white llamas
   B - brown llamas
   C - brown and white llamas
5 B
6 D
7 A and B

PAGES 12-13

1 true
2 false
3 true
4 mountains
5 jungle
6 temple
7 centimetres
8 kilometres

PAGES 14-15

1 January, February, March, April, May, June, July, August, September, October, November, December
2 June
3 100 centimetres
4 50 centimetres
5 300 centimetres
6 less than 30 centimetres

PAGES 16-17

1 A
2 B and C
3 B
4 C
5 odd number
6 8 squirrel monkeys
7 A - 6 monkeys
   B - 6 monkeys
   C - 8 monkeys
   D - 2 monkeys
   E - 4 monkeys

PAGES 18-19

1 there are 26 ants in the box
2 30 ants
3 7 frogs
4 9 frogs
5 13 frogs
6 81, 88, 93, 100 and 300

PAGES 20-21

1 9 millipedes
2 blue morpho butterflies
3 32 poison dart frogs
4 14 centimetres
5 64 + 20 = 84
   20 + 20 = 40
   64 − 20 = 44
   64 + 64 = 128

PAGES 22-23

1 B
2 A - sphere
   B - cube
   C - pyramid
   D - cylinder
3 3 bricks and then 2 bricks
4 1 brick
5 15 bricks

PAGES 24-25

1 Plan A and Plan C
2 6 sections
3 two halves
4 2 quarters
5 1 knot
6 2 knots
7 8 knots

PAGES 26-27

1 4 gold llamas
2 1
3 3
4 13 llama models
5 3 groups
6 3 llamas

PAGES 28-29

1 21, 22, 23, 24 and 25
2 8 = yellow square
   11 = red square
   17 = red square
   20 = yellow square
3 yellow squares
4 A = 6 right angle
   B = 8 right angles
   C = 8 right angles
5 B
6 A